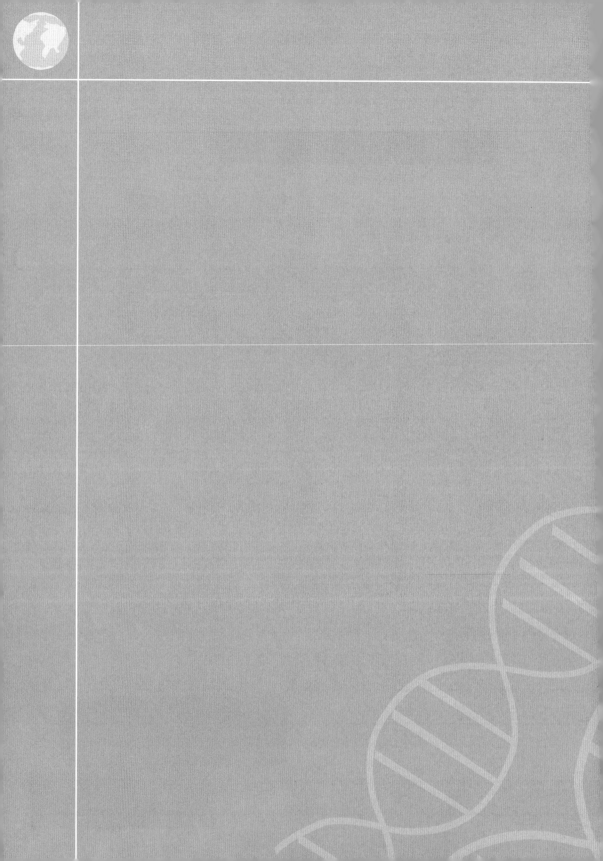

Jane Goodall:
Primatologist and Animal Activist

by Connie Jankowski

Science Contributor
Sally Ride Science
Science Consultants
Thomas R. Ciccone, Science Educator
Ronald Edwards, Ph.D., Science Educator

First hardcover edition published in 2009 by
Compass Point Books
151 Good Counsel Drive
P.O. Box 669
Mankato, MN 56002-0669

Editor: Jennifer VanVoorst
Designer: Heidi Thompson
Editorial Contributor: Sue Vander Hook

Art Director: LuAnn Ascheman-Adams
Creative Director: Joe Ewest
Editorial Director: Nick Healy
Managing Editor: Catherine Neitge

 This book was manufactured with paper containing at least 10 percent post-consumer waste.

Library of Congress Cataloging-in-Publication Data
Jankowski, Connie.
 Jane Goodall : primatologist and animal activist / by Connie Jankowski.
 p. cm. — (Mission: Science)
 ISBN 978-0-7565-4054-8 (library binding)
1. Goodall, Jane, 1934–   —Juvenile literature. 2. Primatologists—England—Biography—
Juvenile literature. 3. Chimpanzees—Tanzania—Gombe Stream National Park—Juvenile literature.
I. Title. II. Series.
 QL31.G58J35 2009
 590.92—dc22
 [B]   2008037621

Visit Compass Point Books on the Internet at *www.compasspointbooks.com*
or e-mail your request to *custserv@compasspointbooks.com*

Table of Contents

Encounter with an Ape

Bananas were missing from Jane Goodall's tent, and she set out to find who took them. Could the thief be one of the chimpanzees she'd been watching at the Gombe Stream Reserve in East Africa?

It didn't take long for Goodall to find an eyewitness. The camp cook had seen it all. He said that David Greybeard, one of the chimpanzees, had entered camp while Goodall was in the forest observing other chimps. For about an hour, the large chimp with the white beard sat in a nearby tree eating fruit. Then he climbed down, walked into Goodall's tent, and took her bananas.

Goodall was excited. It marked a huge breakthrough in her work with the chimps. One of them had finally trusted her enough to come into her camp. David Greybeard returned day after day to eat bananas that Goodall put out for him. After about a month,

he fearlessly took a banana from her hand.

The incident was just the beginning of Goodall's nearly 50-year encounter with the great apes of Africa. She would become the world's leading authority on chimpanzees. And she would provide extraordinary information about their habits, abilities, and social order.

Fun Fact

On Goodall's second birthday, her father gave her a stuffed toy chimp. She named it Jubilee, after a baby chimp she had seen at the London Zoo. To this day, it is one of Goodall's prized possessions.

Goodall on Chimps

Goodall reflected on her life with the chimps: "The long hours spent with them in the forest have enriched my life beyond measure. What I have learned from them has shaped my understanding of human behavior, of our place in nature."

Fascinated with Animals

Valerie Jane Morris-Goodall was born April 3, 1934, in London, England. Four years later, her sister, Judy, was born, completing the Goodall family. When Jane was 5, World War II broke out in Europe, and her father, Mortimer, went off to war. Jane's mother, Vanne, moved the family to a manor owned by her family in Bournemouth in southern England. Shortly after the war, Mortimer and Vanne divorced.

Jane was fascinated with the animals she found in the country. She played with her grandmother's pets, explored the wildlife around her, and rode horses. She dreamed of going to Africa to see the amazing wild animals. Books were her window to Africa. Her favorites were *The Story of Dr. Dolittle* and *Tarzan of the Apes*. By the age of 7, Jane had decided she would someday go to Africa.

HUGH LOFTING
THE STORY OF DR. DOLITTLE

EDGAR RICE BURROUGHS
TARZAN OF THE APES

Cheeta

The Tarzan tales were later made into several movies. The chimpanzee that played Cheeta, Tarzan's friend and companion, was still alive in 2008. At the age of 76, he is the oldest known chimpanzee in the world.

When Jane was 12, she started a four-member nature club called the Alligator Society. Jane, Judy, and two friends did nature projects and played animal games. They also opened a museum and created the *Alligator Society Magazine* with snippets about nature and drawings of insects. Her childhood dreams and ambitions were setting the stage for a lifetime dedicated to animals.

← Both Jane and her sister were interested in animals.

Thanks, Mom!

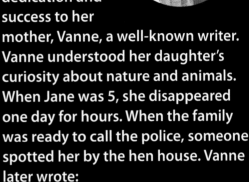

Goodall credits her dedication and success to her mother, Vanne, a well-known writer. Vanne understood her daughter's curiosity about nature and animals. When Jane was 5, she disappeared one day for hours. When the family was ready to call the police, someone spotted her by the hen house. Vanne later wrote:

I don't remember who saw her first—a small, disheveled figure coming a little wearily over the ... field by the hen houses. There were bits of straw in her hair and on her clothes but her eyes, dark ringed with fatigue, were shining.

Jane enthusiastically told her worried family how she had watched silently, without moving, for five hours to see a hen lay an egg. She wanted to know where eggs came from. Although Vanne had been concerned, she was glad her daughter had discovered something so interesting. She would always encourage Jane to accomplish her dreams. She told her to never give up.

When Jane Goodall finished high school, her mother advised her to go to secretarial school. After all, as a secretary, she could get a job anywhere in the world. In 1954, Goodall finished secretarial training and began her first job typing letters at a clinic for children. She held several jobs over the next three years, saving as much money as she could for a trip to Africa. In 1957, at the age of 23, Goodall saw her childhood dream come true. She boarded a ship and traveled to Kenya, Africa, to visit a friend. Her visit would last almost two years.

While in Kenya, Goodall worked at a variety of jobs to support herself. Meanwhile, she explored the countryside and saw animals she had never seen before. And then she met someone who would alter the course of her life. Goodall's friend had told her about Louis Leakey. She set up a meeting with the famous anthropologist—someone who studies the origin and behavior of humans. By chance, Leakey needed a secretary, and Goodall got the job.

Part of her job was traveling with Leakey and his wife, Mary, to dig for human fossils. But Leakey was also interested in studying apes. He thought they would help him understand more about early humans. Goodall wasn't a trained scientist, but Leakey thought that was a good thing. He believed it would make her a perfect candidate for his ape research project. She didn't have any preformed ideas and would be free to observe the facts.

Leakey wanted to know more about apes—their habits, relationships, families, friendships, and enemies. He wanted to know about their ability to think and solve problems. The details would help him compare them to human behavior.

The study would take many years, but Leakey

Louis Leakey (1903–1972)

Louis Leakey was one of the world's greatest archaeologists—someone who digs up and studies the remains of past human life. Leakey learned about early life by examining human skulls, bones, and stone tools. His work convinced many people that the first humans walked in Africa.

Leakey's parents were British missionaries in Kenya, where they lived with an African tribe. Leakey grew up playing and hunting with members of the tribe. He spoke English and the tribal language. At the age of 13, he was initiated as a member of the tribe. At 21, he ventured out on his first fossil exploration, which changed his life. He would go on to study the origin of humans for the rest of his life.

believed Goodall was a special person who could earn the trust of the apes, watch them grow and develop, and study their social interactions. In 1960, Leakey prepared for Goodall to go to the Gombe Stream Reserve near Lake Tanganyika.

"Leakey's Angels"

Louis Leakey is well-known for mentoring three famous female researchers—Jane Goodall, Dian Fossey, and Biruté Galdikas. Later they were dubbed "Leakey's Angels." Each woman studied primates by living with them in their natural habitats. Goodall lived with chimpanzees, while Fossey resided with mountain gorillas and Galdikas with orangutans. They all went on to become significant leaders in primatology.

Living with Chimps

Once Leakey obtained funding and government permission, the path was clear for Jane Goodall to study the chimpanzees at the Gombe Stream Reserve. However, she was not allowed to go alone. Living where wild, strong chimps and other dangerous animals reside could prove dangerous. Jane's mother, Vanne, agreed to go with her. On July 16, 1960, the two women and their African cook arrived at Gombe.

The second day they were there, Jane saw two chimpanzees. It was one of the greatest thrills of her life. The chimps ran whenever they saw her. But she did not give up.

Most days Goodall rose before sunrise. She dressed, ate, and packed food and supplies for her day. Then she quietly waited in the jungle for the chimps to wake up and begin their day. For hours she sat quietly, learning everything she could about the chimps. With binoculars, notebook, and camera in hand, she watched them carefully, recorded their behaviors, and snapped their pictures. She noted how they acted and how they interacted with each other.

When the chimps moved through the jungle, Goodall followed them, sometimes throughout the night. Often it was hard for her to keep up. Vines entangled her feet, steep hills and mountains proved difficult to climb, and sometimes she got separated from the apes.

Did You Know?

Chimps and humans share more than 95 percent of their genes.

Leakey Family Tradition

Louis Leakey's family has established an ongoing tradition of paleontology over the past century. Louis and his second wife, Mary Douglas Leakey, were world-famous fossil hunters. Their son Richard continued his parents' work and became well-known for discovering a 1.6 million-year-old skeleton. Richard and his wife, fellow researcher Meave Epps Leakey, are among the most famous paleontologists in the world. Along with their daughter Louise Leakey, they continue the family tradition by leading expeditions together. The Leakeys' work as the most important paleontologists in history still continues today.

As time went on, the chimps became more accustomed to Goodall's presence. She slowly inched nearer to the apes every day. She watched mothers groom their babies and adult chimps groom each other—a sign of affection and respect. Goodall observed their kindness as well as their conflicts. Before long, she could recognize each chimp by looks and behavior. Instead of assigning each one a number, as scientists generally did, she gave them names. One she called David Greybeard, while another large chimp was named Goliath. Some of the others were dubbed Fifi, Flo, and Otta.

Goodall tried to earn the chimps' trust and fit in with the group. She kept as quiet as possible, learning to act like the chimps. Patiently she waited for them to accept her, and finally the chimps became comfortable with her presence. They allowed her to sit nearby, and she began discovering important things about chimps that no one had ever known before. It was a huge breakthrough when David Greybeard visited Goodall's tent in the summer of 1961.

In October Goodall made a surprising discovery. She

Goodall waited patiently until the chimpanzees let her get close. Sometimes the chimps got really close, too!

saw a male chimp eating a piece of meat while the other chimps sat around looking longingly at his prize. Scientists had long believed that chimpanzees were mostly vegetarians, eating insects and rodents occasionally. But Goodall saw that they also clearly ate meat from sizable animals. Later she would observe them hunting bushpigs, very hairy pigs that live in dense forests or jungles. As important as that discovery was, it would not be Goodall's most significant finding.

About Chimps

- Chimps don't like to be in water; most cannot swim.
- Chimps do not have tails.
- Chimps are quadrupedal, which means they walk on all four limbs; they can also walk upright for short distances.
- At birth, chimps weigh about 4 pounds (1.8 kilograms).
- Adult chimps stand about 4 feet (120 centimeters) high; males weigh from 90 to 120 pounds (40 to 54 kg), and females weigh from 60 to 110 pounds (27 to 50 kg).
- About 50 chimps usually live together in a community led by the alpha (most dominant) male; the group patrols its territory strictly; conflicts can occur with neighboring groups.
- Chimps can recognize themselves in a mirror.
- Chimps rarely live past the age of 50 in the wild, but they have been known to reach more than 70 years old in captivity.

Did You Know?

Ethology is the scientific study of animal behavior, especially in the animal's natural habitat.

A month later, in November 1961, Goodall made one of her most important discoveries. She observed the chimps making and using tools to get food. She saw David Greybeard and Goliath stripping leaves from a branch. Then they used the branch as a tool to fish termites out of their mounds, the tall strong nests where the insects hide. The chimps pushed the bare branch into the mound and waited for termites to crawl onto it. Then they pulled out their snack, a branch full of clinging termites.

Goodall watched the chimps use rocks or sticks to break open fruit. They also used leaves to scoop up drinking water. Why was this so important? Until that point, making tools was believed to be something only humans could do. Now scientists had to change their definition of "human." And they realized that chimps are more intelligent than they had previously thought.

The discoveries Goodall was making in the Gombe Stream Reserve were reshaping and changing scientists' understanding of anthropology and ethology. She saw that chimps each had their own personalities with sharp minds and varying emotions. They formed families and interacted socially with each other.

Goodall's work soon became known all over the world. Wildlife photographers arrived from *National Geographic* magazine to capture the amazing things going on at the Gombe Stream Reserve. In August 1963, *National Geographic* published the photos along with Goodall's account of her experience, "My Life Among Wild Chimpanzees." The whole world was talking about this woman who lived with the apes.

Goodall observed chimpanzees using tools to get food.

17

Jane Goodall was receiving international fame, but she realized that most scientists wouldn't take her findings seriously because she didn't have a college degree. So Louis Leakey talked to officials at Cambridge University in England and got permission for Goodall to attend as a doctoral student. It was very unusual for a university to allow someone to work on a Ph.D. without first having a college degree. While Goodall was in England taking classes, visiting students carried on her work with the chimps at Gombe. In 1965, Goodall was awarded a doctorate in ethology.

In 1964, the year before Goodall earned her Ph.D., she married Hugo van Lawick, one of *National Geographic*'s wildlife photographers. They had met in 1962 when van Lawick came to Gombe to photograph Goodall and the chimps. Now they worked together in Gombe and other parts of Africa.

A happy event occurred at Gombe on March 4, 1967. Goodall gave birth to a son, Hugo Eric Louis van Lawick. Goodall called him "Grub." She now spent less time studying and writing about the chimpanzees so she could spend time with her son. Although she still worked at the reserve, Goodall and her husband bought a home in the nearby suburbs of Nairobi. Students took over much of the work with the chimpanzees.

The 1970s was a decade of change for Goodall. She and her husband spent less time together and eventually divorced in 1974. The next year, Goodall married Derek Bryceson, whom she had met earlier at the Gombe Stream Reserve. He was the director of Tanzania National Park. He died from cancer in 1980.

As Goodall became more well-known, she became a popular speaker for groups all over the world. In 1971,

Goodall and her son, Grub

Stanford University in California asked her to become a visiting professor. Twice a year, she traveled to the university to lecture and mentor students.

In 1975, a terrorist group ravaged the Gombe camp and kidnapped four people—three Stanford students and one staff member. Others were quickly evacuated. Goodall worked with government officials and wrote letters to help free the hostages. Eventually all were released.

The camp was no longer a safe place, so in 1976, Goodall sent Grub to England to live with her mother. Goodall continued her work at Gombe. That year the Jane Goodall Institute for Wildlife Research was established. Goodall's work would be supported into the future.

▲ Goodall posed with the staff of the Jane Goodall Institute in Gombe National Park, Tanzania.

Lesser Apes and Great Apes

Many people confuse apes with monkeys. They are different in many ways. Monkeys are usually smaller and swing through the trees using their long tails. Apes have no tails and use their long arms to either swing from tree to tree or walk. Apes are divided into two groups: lesser apes and great apes. Lesser apes, which are smaller than the great apes and live in the rain forests, include gibbons and siamang. With great strength and quickness, they swing through the trees, grasping one branch after another. Great apes include gorillas, chimpanzees, and orangutans. They move about mostly by knuckle-walking on the ground. Orangutans swing slowly through the trees.

Dian Fossey
(1932—1985)

The year Goodall received her doctorate, Dian Fossey—the second of "Leakey's Angels"—began her work with primates. She spent her first year in Zaire, Africa (now the Democratic Republic of Congo) studying gorillas. But political turmoil drove her out of the country and into Rwanda where she would observe gorillas for 18 years.

Fossey had been interested in animals from an early age. When she first went to college, she wanted to become a veterinarian. But she changed her major and became an occupational therapist in Kentucky. In 1963, Fossey took a safari vacation to Africa, which would change her life. There she met Louis Leakey, who sparked her interest in apes. She went back to her job, but returned to Africa in 1966 to live with the gorillas.

Like Goodall, Fossey became part of the apes' world. She observed their travels and habits. But she also saw poachers come into the area and kill the gorillas or capture them to sell to zoos. Some gorillas were injured and left to die. So Fossey set up a makeshift medical center to treat their wounds. She nursed them back to health as best she could and cared for two orphaned baby gorillas.

In time, Fossey learned to communicate with the gorillas. One of the most memorable moments of her work was when a male gorilla reached out and touched her hand. This was the first recorded friendly act from a gorilla to a human. Fossey became a strong supporter of humane treatment of gorillas. In 1983, she wrote *Gorillas in the Mist,* a book about her experiences. In 1988, her book was made into the film *Gorillas in the Mist: The Story of Dian Fossey.*

In 1985, Fossey was found murdered in her mountain cabin. Her death is unsolved, but poachers are suspected. She is buried next to her favorite gorilla, Digit, who was beheaded by poachers in 1978. Her gravestone reads: "No one loved gorillas more."

Jane Goodall spent decades in the jungle. She observed the birth of chimpanzee babies and watched them grow up and live out their lives. Always amazed by what they could do, Goodall noted their intelligence and athletic abilities. She recorded everything she discovered about these long-armed great apes with their deep bonds between mother and child, as well as between some siblings.

Her notes also included disease, death, and cruelty. Ten years after Goodall's arrival at Gombe, she saw a disturbing side of the chimpanzees she had grown to love. Her community of chimp families began warring against each other. They divided into two groups of male chimps. Goodall called them the Kasakelas and the Kahamas. They grew to hate each other and continued fighting for years. By 1977, the last Kahama male was dead, ending the long war between the chimps.

Chimpanzees form strong social ➡ bonds, just like humans.

Goodall had so much to share with the world. Each night at Gombe Stream Reserve, she copied her daily notes into journals and made charts of the chimps' changing behaviors. She organized and labeled her photos. On a typewriter, she pounded out her story—the account of her life among the chimpanzees.

Goodall would eventually write several books of her adventures, including *My Life With the Chimpanzees*, *Through a Window*, and *In the Shadow of Man*. Her autobiography is called *Africa in My Blood: An Autobiography in Letters: The Early Years*. In *Through a Window*, Goodall presented life stories of many of the chimps. She described the power plays of a chimp that always wanted to dominate the others. And she wrote about mother chimps, their babies, and the numerous tragedies and triumphs in the jungle.

▲ A young chimpanzee spends the first seven to 10 years of its life by its mother's side.

Sick Chimps

The chimpanzees at Gombe got some of the same diseases as humans. They suffered from colds and flu. But in 1966, a polio epidemic hit some nearby villages. Polio is caused by a virus that attacks nerve cells in the brain and spinal cord. Severe cases can cause permanent paralysis. Some of the chimps were afflicted with the disease. Four chimps died, and others became paralyzed. When a vaccine became available, Goodall shot doses of it into the bananas she gave to the chimps. This protected many of them from the disease.

In 1984, Jane Goodall received the J. Paul Getty Wildlife Conservation Prize. She received the award for "helping millions of people understand the importance of wildlife conservation to life on this planet." That year she launched Chimpanzoo, a program to apply first-rate research methods for chimpanzees in captivity.

Goodall also became interested in conditions for chimps at research

laboratories throughout the world. In 1986, she received a copy of a film secretly taken at Sema, Inc., in Rockville, Maryland, where about 500 primates were used for scientific research. Conditions for the chimps were disgusting, and Goodall knew she had to try to help them. In 1987, she toured Sema and was horrified at how the chimps were living. She visited other research labs. Some had poor conditions like Sema, while others treated the animals with great care.

Goodall set out to make sure that all chimpanzees were treated humanely. She wrote articles and talked about it whenever she spoke. She said, "The least I can do is speak out for those who cannot speak for themselves."

At a conference in Chicago, she learned about another threat to chimpanzees. Other speakers described how African habitats were being destroyed. The habitats of chimpanzees were now in danger. Rain forests were being cut down to use the wood for furniture or clear the land for farms. Places where chimps once thrived were now dying. Chimps were also being killed for food. Baby chimps were being sold to zoos or to individuals as pets. Goodall wrote, "I can never forget the first time I saw one of these pathetic infants for sale in the tourist market of a Central African town."

Goodall with children in the ➡ Roots & Shoots program

Hunting and selling chimps is illegal, but no one was doing anything about it. But Goodall did something. She contacted authorities who rescued this little chimp that she had named Little Jay. Goodall still actively works to make life better for chimpanzees everywhere.

Roots & Shoots

In 1991, on her back porch, Goodall met with 16 Tanzanian teenagers who were concerned about their community, animals, and the environment. They expressed fears for the future such as pollution, deforestation, and the survival of animals such as Goodall's beloved chimpanzees. These were topics that weren't included in their school curriculum. The teens organized a program called Roots & Shoots to fill the gaps and address the problems. In 1993, chapters were organized in the United States and Europe.

Continued Efforts

In 2002, Jane Goodall received a special honor. United Nations Secretary-General Kofi Annan appointed her to serve as a U.N. Messenger of Peace. Goodall travels the world and writes articles and books that will help animals and preserve their environments.

Goodall has spent nearly 50 years of her lifetime studying chimpanzees. Through her teaching, lectures, and organizations, she promotes her cause to protect chimps and other animals and save them from extinction. Her passion that began as a young girl is still strong.

Although her home is now in England, Goodall still visits her beloved chimp families in Africa. Now in her 70s, she continues to tell the world how to better care for Earth's animals and their habitats. Through her work with chimps, Jane Goodall truly works for all of us.

Awards and Honors

Jane Goodall has received many awards for her years of research. Among them are the National Geographic Society's Hubbard Medal, the Albert Schweitzer Award from the Animal Welfare Institute in Washington, D.C., and Japan's Kyoto Prize in Basic Science.

Goodall at the United Nations ▼

In Danger of Extinction

Long ago there were dinosaurs, and now there are none. Animals such as the dodo bird, the giant ground sloth, the saber-toothed cat, and the Tasmanian tiger used to make their homes on Earth. But they are now extinct—none of them exist anymore.

Other animals are considered endangered and at risk of extinction. Goodall's beloved chimpanzees are among this group. Still others are considered threatened, which means they are likely to be endangered in the near future. Some animals were endangered species but are now recovering because of efforts to protect them and their habitats.

The following animals are just a few of the many endangered animals today:

- African elephant
- gorilla
- Bengal tiger
- chimpanzee
- cougar
- great white shark

Primatologist: Biruté Galdikas

Simon Fraser University, British Columbia

What would it be like to live with orangutans? Ask Biruté Galdikas, who has lived with this endangered species and studied them for 35 years. Galdikas took up residence with the orangutans in the jungles of Borneo in Southeast Asia. She tracks them through the forests and watches them closely.

When Galdikas was a young girl, her first library book was *Curious George*. The story made her ask important questions: "Why are we here? What are we doing here? Who are we?" Her fascination with apes grew, and she focused her interests on the orangutan, a big, red, long-armed, intelligent, hairy ape.

Galdikas first met anthropologist Louis Leakey at the University

Did You Know?

Galdikas discovered that orangutans collect and eat more than 400 types of food, including fruit, nuts, bark, and bugs.

of California, Los Angeles, when she was a graduate student in the early 1970s. She told Leakey of her desire to study the orangutan and convinced him to help her research them in their habitat.

In 1971, Galdikas arrived at the Tanjung Putting Reserve in Borneo. The research camp was set up with the help of Leakey and the National Geographic Society. Galdikas became known as the third of "Leakey's Angels," following Jane Goodall and Dian Fossey.

Galdikas once said, "When you look into orangutans' eyes, they look like human beings in red suits." She has made friends with the large apes over the years and is recognized as an authority on orangutans. "This is what I was meant to do," she has said.

Name:	Jane Goodall (born Valerie Jane Morris-Goodall)
Date of birth:	April 3, 1934
Nationality:	British
Birthplace:	London, England
Parents:	Mortimer Morris-Goodall
	Margaret "Vanne" Myfanwe Morris-Goodall
Spouses:	Hugo van Lawick (1937–2002)
	Derek Bryceson (1923–1980)
Children:	Hugo Eric Louis van Lawick (1967–)
Field of study:	Ethology, primatology, conservation
Known for:	Study of chimpanzees' behaviors and social and family interactions in Gombe Stream Reserve, Tanzania, Africa
Contributions to science:	Discovered that chimpanzees make their own tools and eat meat
Awards and honors:	J. Paul Getty Wildlife Conservation Prize, 1984; Kyoto Prize in Basic Science, 1990; National Geographic Society Hubbard Medal for Distinction in Exploration, Discovery, and Research, 1995; United Nations Messenger of Peace appointment, 2002; Dame of the British Empire, 2003; 60th Anniversary Medal of UNESCO and the French Legion of Honor, 2006; honorary doctorate from the University of Liverpool, 2007
Publications:	*My Friends the Wild Chimpanzees; My Life With the Chimpanzees; Through a Window; In the Shadow of Man; Africa in My Blood: An Autobiography in Letters: The Early Years; The Chimpanzees of Gombe: Patterns of Behavior, 1986; 40 Years at Gombe, 2000*

Francis Maitland Balfour (1851–1882)
British zoologist who made several suggestions for animal classification, including that animals with backbones be classed as Chordata, a term that is still used today

Caspar Bauhin (1560–1624)
Swiss botanist who developed the use of genus and species names for classification

Pierre Belon (1517–1564)
French naturalist who determined that many species had skeletal similarities; classified more than 200 species and compared the bones of humans and birds

Charles Robert Darwin (1809–1882)
British naturalist who revolutionized biology with his theory of evolution through the process of natural selection

Charles Benedict Davenport (1866–1944)
American zoologist and geneticist who introduced statistics into evolutionary studies

Edward Forbes (1815–1854)
British naturalist who was the first to propose that living organisms exist deep in the oceans, below where light penetrates

Dian Fossey (1932–1985)
American zoologist who studied gorillas in the mountain forests of Rwanda, Africa; mentored by archaeologist Louis Leakey; wrote *Gorillas in the Mist*; murdered at the age of 53 in her mountain cabin in Rwanda

Karl von Frisch (1886–1982)
Austrian zoologist who studied animal behavior, especially communication among bees

Biruté Galdikas (1946–   )
Anthropologist who for 35 years has studied and lived with orangutans in the jungles of Borneo in Southeast Asia

Étienne Geoffroy Saint-Hilaire (1772–1844)
French naturalist who described most of the known animals of his time

Theodore Nicholas Gill (1837–1914)
American ichthyologist (scientist who studies fish) and outstanding taxonomist of his time, who had a major influence on the field of ichthyology

Louis Leakey (1903–1972)
Archaeologist and explorer who studied fossils and stone tools in Africa and learned about early humans; convinced scientists that the first humans walked in Africa; mentor to Jane Goodall, Dian Fossey, and Biruté Galdikas

Carolus Linnaeus (1707–1778)
Swedish naturalist who introduced certain classifications of organisms that are still in use today

Ernst Walter Mayr (1904–2005)
German-born American zoologist who performed numerous studies on classification of organisms

John Ray (1628–1705)
British naturalist and taxonomist who first proposed the concept of species; helped to lay the groundwork for classification systems

Georg Wilhelm Steller (1709–1746)
German naturalist and explorer who studied numerous species, including the Steller's jay, sea lion, and eider duck

Sir Charles Wyville Thomson (1830–1882)
British marine biologist who determined that life exists deep in the oceans

Nikolaas Tinbergen (1907–1988)
Dutch-born British zoologist who studied animal behavior under natural conditions

Francis Willughby (1635–1672)
British naturalist who presented a systematic work on birds and fish, paving the way for Linnaeus' classification

Alexander Wilson (1706–1813)
British-born American who was the founder of ornithology (the study of birds) in America; drew and wrote about birds and noted 48 species previously unknown in the United States

Glossary

anthropologist—scientist who studies the origin of humans, including behavior and culture

behavior—actions of a person or animal in response to things around him or her

conservation—protection, preservation, and management of wildlife and nature

environment—circumstances surrounding an organism or group of organisms, including physical and abstract features

ethology—science of animal behavior

extinction—becoming extinct; no longer in existence

gene—unit of a cell that determines the characteristics an offspring inherits from its parents

habitat—environment in which an animal normally lives

mentored—gave another person help and advice over a period of time or taught the person how to do a job

paleontologist—scientist who studies prehistoric life

poacher—one who illegally hunts or fishes, usually on someone else's property

primate—mammal of the order Primate, characterized by highly developed hands and feet, a shortened face, and a large brain

primatologist—scientist who studies primates

social—living together in groups

taxonomist—scientist who studies organisms for the purpose of classification into an ordered system

veterinarian—medical doctor who cares for animals

1934	Valerie Jane Morris-Goodall is born April 3
1939	At the age of 5, she watches a hen for five hours to see it lay an egg
1941	Decides at the age of 7 that she must go to Africa someday
1946	Starts a four-member nature club called the Alligator Society, opens a museum, and creates the *Alligator Society Magazine*
1954	Finishes secretarial training and begins her first job typing letters at a clinic for children
1957	Travels to Kenya, Africa, to visit a friend; meets Louis Leakey and begins working as his secretary
1960	Arrives at Gombe Stream Reserve near Lake Tanganyika in East Africa on July 16 with her mother and African cook
1961	David Greybeard, one of the chimpanzees, visits Goodall's tent in the summer and steals her bananas; in October, she observes a male chimp eating a piece of meat, showing that chimps are not solely vegetarians; in November, she discovers that chimps make and use tools, an ability scientists had previously reserved for humans
1962	Photographers from *National Geographic* magazine come to Gombe to photograph Goodall and the chimpanzees
1963	*National Geographic* magazine publishes her story, "My Life Among Wild Chimpanzees," along with vivid pictures of the apes
1964	Marries Hugo van Lawick, one of *National Geographic*'s wildlife photographers
1965	Receives a doctoral degree from Cambridge University in England; students carry on her work at Gombe

1966	Polio epidemic hits nearby villages; some of the chimps get the polio virus and are permanently paralyzed
1967	Gives birth to a son, Hugo Eric Louis van Lawick; nicknames him "Grub"
1971	Observes cannibalism among the chimps; male chimps divide into two groups and war against each other
1974	Divorces Hugo van Lawick
1975	Marries Derek Bryceson; a terrorist group attacks the Gombe camp and kidnaps three students and one staff member
1976	Sends her son, Grub, to England to live with his grandmother; establishes the Jane Goodall Institute for Wildlife Research
1977	The war between the chimps ends when the last male of the Kahama group is killed
1984	Receives the J. Paul Getty Wildlife Conservation Prize; launches Chimpanzoo, a program to monitor research for chimpanzees in captivity
1986	Sees film taken at Sema, Inc. and determines to help improve conditions for chimps used for medical research; leads to efforts to protect chimps from being captured and sold, and to save their habitats that are being destroyed
1991	Meets with 16 Tanzanian teenagers who establish Roots & Shoots, a youth organization to address concerns about animals and the environment
2002	Appointed as a U.N. Messenger of Peace by United Nations Secretary-General Kofi Annan.
2008	Awarded the Montana State University Medal for Global and Visionary Leadership

Goodall, Jane. *My Life With the Chimpanzees*. New York: Pocket Books, 1996.

Goodall, Jane. *Chimpanzees I Love: Saving Their World and Ours*. New York: Scholastic Press, 2001.

Haugen, Brenda. *Jane Goodall: Legendary Primatologist*. Minneapolis: Compass Point Books, 2006.

McGhee, Karen, and George McKay. *Encyclopedia of Animals*. Washington, D.C.: National Geographic, 2007.

Stonehouse, Bernard, and Esther Bertram. *How Animals Live: The Amazing World of Animals in the Wild*. New York: Scholastic, 2004.

On the Web

For more information on this topic, use FactHound.

1. Go to *www.facthound.com*
2. Choose your grade level.
3. Begin your search.

This book's ID number is 9780756540548

FactHound will find the best sites for you.

Connie Jankowski

Connie Jankowski is a seasoned journalist, marketing expert, public relations consultant, and teacher. Her education includes a bachelor of arts from the University of Pittsburgh and graduate study at Pitt. She has worked in publishing, public relations, and marketing for the past 25 years. Jankowski is the author of 11 books and hundreds of magazine articles.